CORGIS

FAVORITE DOG BREEDS

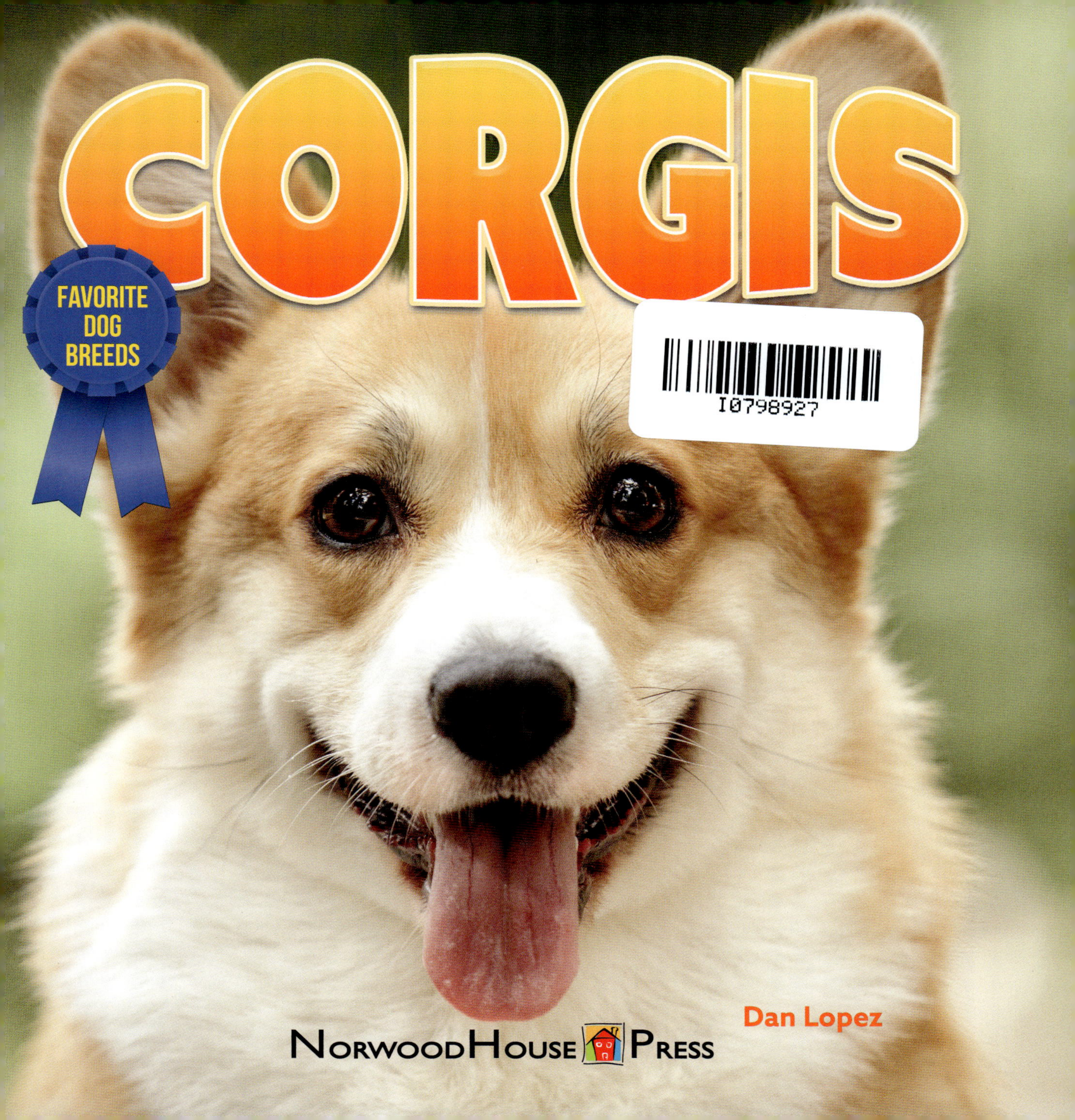

Dan Lopez

NorwoodHouse Press

Cataloging-in-Publication Data

Names: Lopez, Dan.
Title: Corgis / Dan Lopez.
Description: Buffalo, NY : Norwood House Press, 2026. | Series: Favorite dog breeds| Includes glossary and index.
Identifiers: ISBN 9781978576568 (pbk.) | ISBN 9781978576575 (library bound) | ISBN 9781978576582 (ebook)
Subjects: LCSH: Pembroke Welsh corgi--Juvenile literature. | Cardigan Welsh corgi--Juvenile literature
Classification: LCC SF429.P33 L67 2026 | DDC 636.737--dc23

Published in 2026 by
Norwood House Press
2544 Clinton Street
Buffalo, NY 14224

Designer: Rhea Magaro
Editor: Kim Thompson

Photo credits:
Cover, p. 1 Natalia Fedosova, Giraphics/Shutterstock.com; p. 4 Library of Congress; p. 5 sergey kolesnikov/Shutterstock.com; p. 6 ZARIN ANDREY/Shutterstock.com; p. 7 Nan Liu/Shutterstock.com; p. 8 Vera Reva/Shutterstock.com; p. 10 ANNA TITOVA/Shutterstock.com; p. 11 Lyntree/Shutterstock.com; p. 13 OlesyaPogosskaya/Shutterstock.com; p. 14 Inessa Melikova/Shutterstock.com; p. 16 Pixel-Shot/Shutterstock.com; p. 17 Lmnovak/Shutterstock.com; p. 19 otsphoto/Shutterstock.com; p. 20 Pixel-Shot/Shutterstock.com; p. 21 MDavidova/Shutterstock.com

Printed in the United States of America

CPSIA compliance information: Batch #CWNHP26: For further information contact Norwood House Press at 1-800-237-9932.

TABLE OF CONTENTS

Meet the Corgi

Welsh corgis are popular pets. They are known for their short **stature**, tall ears, and friendliness.

Queen Elizabeth II was famous for owning corgis. She had more than 30 during her life.

What Do Corgis Look Like?

Corgis have short legs and long, **stocky** bodies.

They stand 10 to 12 inches (25 to 30 centimeters) tall. They weigh 24 to 30 pounds (11 to 14 kilograms).

A corgi's coat can be black, tan, red, **sable**, or **fawn**. Most corgis have white markings. The corgi's upright ears make it look a little like a fox.

There are two **breeds** of Welsh corgis. The Pembroke has a shorter coat. It has a short tail and ears that are more pointed.

Pembroke Welsh Corgi

Cardigan Welsh Corgi

The Cardigan has a longer coat. It has a long tail and large, rounded ears.

Where Do Corgis Come From?

Corgis come from the country of Wales. It is part of the United Kingdom.

In the Welsh language, *corgi* means “dog.”

Corgis were bred to **herd** farm animals. Their short legs let them run under the larger animals. Corgis nip at the animals' legs to make them move.

Do Corgis Make Good Pets?

Corgis make great pets. They are smart, **affectionate**, and full of energy. Corgis are cute when they sploot. This means they lie on their bellies with their legs stretched out.

Corgis are very **loyal** to their families. They can be **territorial**. They might try to chase away dogs they don't know.

What Do Corgis Need?

Corgis need two meals a day. They **shed** a lot, so they need lots of brushing.

Corgis are very active. They need at least one hour of exercise every day.

Glossary

affectionate (uh-FEK-shuh-nit): loving and caring

breeds (breedz): different types of the same kind of animal

fawn (fawn): a light brown color like the color of a young deer's coat

herd (hurd): to move animals from one place to another by guiding them

loyal (LOI-uhl): faithful and true to someone or something

sable (SAY-buhl): a dark brown color that looks almost black

shed (shed): to lose hair or fur naturally

stature (STACH-ur): how tall something is; height

stocky (STAH-kee): having a short, thick, and strong body

territorial (ter-i-TOR-ee-uhl): wanting to protect your own home or area from others

Thinking Questions

1. Describe a corgi's ears.
2. What are the two breeds of Welsh corgis?
3. Where is Wales?
4. How does a corgi's body help it herd farm animals?
5. Describe a corgi's personality.

Index

About the Author

Dan Lopez is a writer who loves dogs! He has a German shepherd named Hans and an Irish setter named Tam. They love to go for walks in the woods together. Sometimes, they jump in the lake for a swim. Dan lives in Indiana with his wife and three kids.